Your Heart's Desire
A Loving Relationship

Ken Keyes, Jr.

LIVING LOVE PUBLICATIONS
Coos Bay, Oregon

This book may be obtained through your local bookstore. Or you may order it from Living Love Publications, 790 Commercial Avenue, Coos Bay, Oregon 97420, for $3.95 plus $1.25 for postage and packing.

International Standard Book Number
0-915972-05-0

Library of Congress Cataloging in Publication Data
Keyes, Ken.
    Your heart's desire.
    1. Love. 2. Love--Psychological aspects.
I. Title.
HQ801.K49   1983   646.7'8   83-19924
ISBN 0-915972-05-0 (pbk.)

First Printing, October 1983. 15,000 copies.
Second Printing, December 1984, 15,000 copies.

LIVING LOVE PUBLICATIONS
790 Commercial Avenue
Coos Bay, Oregon 97420

*This book is dedicated
to the future of
all humanity—
whose survival depends
on rapidly increasing our skill
in creating loving relationships
as couples,
in organizations,
and between nations.*

ACKNOWLEDGEMENTS

This book has been produced by a team of dedicated people. My special thanks and appreciation go to Britta Zetterberg, the Director of Living Love Publications, for the work she so generously put into editing and expanding this book. Because of the extent of her contribution, I asked Britta to coauthor the book with me, but she declined.

I also want to acknowledge the useful feedback from Peggy Wallace, Jude Houston, Debbie Ham and Gerda Lawrence. Carole Finley lovingly made the drawings at the end of each chapter.

And finally, I wish to acknowledge the help of Penny Hannig, with whom I've been in a relationship for almost five years. Her suggestions, which always bring greater clarity to the pages, and the support that she continually offers me, have given me the energy to write my latest five books in only five years.

Ken Keyes, Jr.
Coos Bay, Oregon

Contents

INTRODUCTION

Few people know many couples who truly get along
well with each other for a lifetime. We even joke
about it: "Marriage made them one—and they
spent the rest of their lives fighting about who was
the one!"

My own experience was no better, and so I started
hunting for the answers that I sorely needed. After
two divorces, I wanted to find the key that would
open the door to a harmonious relationship.
My marriages were probably about 90% the way
I wanted them, but I was stuck on wanting perfection
and I let that missing 10% ruin the beauty of the rest.

I came to realize that love is not just a wonderful
feeling that will remain with us forever after
Cupid wraps a warm glow around us. Love is a deep
heart space that is maintained by a determination
to make the relationship work. To bring the magic of
enduring love into our lives, we must work on
changing outdated ways of reacting.

In this book I want to share with you the ways in
which I have created security, comfort and enjoyment
by loving unconditionally. From this deep well of
love, I can increasingly cope with all the shifting
circumstances of life.

The strategy I will describe starts with:

. . . becoming aware of how we have arrived at our
current ways of looking at ourselves and our relationships, our specific desires and ideas of perfection
to which we cling.

. . . then observing how the different parts within us are trying to fulfill those desires in more or less skillful ways,

. . . and learning to look for our positive intentions to find love and appreciation behind our thoughts and actions,

. . . and finally becoming ever more expert at listening attentively to the messages from our partners. We can learn to sift out that which is part of their defense system and to tune-in to the yearning for love within them.

By using and testing the ideas I present here, I have become clear on how I can create my experience of a loving relationship. And I have discovered that it is possible to live happily with a partner who does not meet all my models about how she should feel and act.

One key in the process of creating a loving relationship is to learn to define the priorities: to realize that love is more important than being right, being fair, being successful or rich. Another key is to be able to let go of demands for fairness, logic, efficiency, etc. in favor of unconditional love. This process leads me to my heart's desire—a loving relationship with unlimited levels of enjoyment and fulfillment—no matter what happens in the drama of my life.

Coos Bay Oregon   Ken Keyes, Jr.
August, 1983

Myth and
Mental Habits

Does the myth of romance
still have you in its grip
with expectations
of permanent bliss?

Do you feel like a failure
and blame your partner or yourself
if you no longer recapture
the enthusiasm and joy
of the ecstatic days
when you first fell in love?

Do you feel
that promises have been broken,
that your dreams have been shattered
and that your relationship
is not working?

You can take heart
and know that
falling in love
is just nature's way
of luring you
into a relationship.

The blinding rush
of romantic love
is not a solid basis
for your union.

With its sexual attraction
and rush of infatuation,
it temporarily conceals
many differences and problems.

It may make you ignore warning signs
and become overconfident
about your ability
to bypass roadblocks.

onor romance
for bringing you together
with your beloved,
for giving you a sample
of the mystical ecstasy
that is available
in a lifetime of loving.

After the bloom of romance fades
and the differences begin to emerge
the opportunity is open
for real love.

Now is the time
to make a conscious choice
to devote your energy
to the nurturing of your beloved
and yourself.

It is time
to face the differences between you
with courage (and even interest),
to learn from each other,
to be open
and determined
to maintain a heart space.

Above all, it is time to expose
the true villain in the drama:
our demands and expectations
that we ourselves,
our partners
and the world at large
must behave in a certain way
so that we can be happy.

These demands are a result
of our common needs for survival
as well as our desires
for comfort and approval.

They result from
our value systems,
our particular ideals
of success,
beauty, truth and goodness.

From earliest childhood,
when our needs and desires
were not met,
we built up defenses
to protect ourselves—
defenses based on whatever skills
we had at each moment.

A baby has no other choice
than to cry when it wants
food, warmth and comfort.

A 5-year-old may have few options,
other than withdrawal and fear,
when repeatedly scolded
by a beloved mother—
a mother whose frustrations
may be totally unrelated
to any actions of the child.

One child, unfairly accused
by an adored parent,
will feel deeply hurt
and hang on to the painful memory.

Another will strike out
in self-defense
and receive ridicule—or more abuse.

9

Over the years,
similar events
will reopen these wounds
and end up leaving scars
in the mind of the adult.

We manage to weave
an intricate web of core beliefs,
demands and expectations
that reflect our life experiences,
beliefs inflicted by painful events
and by parents
and others who themselves
are driven by conditioning
from their own childhoods.

We internalize our own mixture
of thoughts such as:

- It is dangerous to trust.

- It isn't safe to get close.

- It isn't safe to honestly
  express my feelings.

- The world owes me a good life.

- No one believes in me.

- I can't afford to be seen as I am.

- I have to please at all costs.

- It would be awful
  if I made a mistake.

- I have to do good deeds
  to be worthwhile.

- I must be competent or talented
  in some important area.

11

- I have to pay my way
  or nobody will love me.

- I must have love or validation
  from all the people
  who are significant to me.

- It doesn't matter what I do—
  I'll never succeed anyway.

- Life is unfair—
  there is no justice in the world.

- I'm no good.

- I never do anything right.

- I don't deserve happiness.

- I can't change the feelings
  and behavior I acquired in the past.

We find ourselves,
as adults,
still living
with stereotyped ways
of thinking and reacting,
often developed
when we felt hurt or injured;
even though our responses
do not serve
the intended purpose
of alleviating
the pain.

By constant repetition
we have programmed ourselves
into believing
that these concepts
are real, true and unchangeable.

13

As adults we have the ability
to break the vicious cycle.

We can become aware
of our unworkable programming
and refuse to perpetuate it.

We can know:
behind all of our demands,
and all of our defense mechanisms,
lie fears—
the fear of being alone,
of not being good enough,
of not being worthy of love.

Within each of us
is the deep longing
to feel good about ourselves
and to be appreciated
and loved by others.

Almost all of us
have had a taste
of what love and acceptance
is like.

We treasure the special moments
when we have felt a deep union,
and a closeness in body,
mind and spirit.

We cherish these moments—
full of magic and warmth,
serenity and ecstasy,
satisfaction and bliss.

Hidden deep within our beings
is a longing
to recreate these moments.

Now let's follow the route
that can lead us
to our heart's desire.

2

The Road
to Happiness

Few of us use
the direct route
to find the love
and appreciation
for which
we so deeply long.

17

Too often we use
complicated, indirect routes
that confuse and frustrate us
when they don't work.

Indirect routes
involve striving for
what we think we must have
in order to deserve or get
what we *really* want.

We're taught that appreciating
and loving ourselves
just because we're here and alive
is conceited and wrong.

We must be a certain way
to earn love.

Each culture offers
a myriad of messages
about what we must do
to be loved.

One may think,
"If I get a good education,
live in the 'right' part of town,
am successful financially
and travel to glamorous places,
people will respect me
and I'll find
an attractive partner.
Then I will be happy."

For most of my life
I used that route myself.

I sought
prestige and admiration
in the hope of feeding
the longing void within.

19

My ego-mind thought
that if I had the "right" partner,
we would almost always
want the same things.

When this did not happen
I kept looking
for that "perfect" partner
who could fulfill my desires.

I seldom expressed
my deepest feelings
(unless they made me look good
or I was emotionally exploding).

I emphasized
"me" and "mine"
rather than
"us" and "ours."

I tuned-in to
the tide of permissiveness
that tries to make
sexual adventure with others
compatible with a happy marriage.

21

In these and other ways
I created separateness
and denied the part of me
that longs for deeper love,
togetherness
and unity.

I tried to manipulate my partner
into changing
to fit my model
of perfection.

When she opposed me
I found subtle ways
to coerce her
or to make her pay
for her "stubbornness."

My ego took the position
that unless I got sex,
when I wanted it,
the way I wanted it,
I would look elsewhere.

I constantly offered
criticism, analysis and advice—
adding my "words of wisdom"
when she was moody or upset,
and needing understanding instead.

I often withheld
compliments, validation,
spontaneous gifts
and a helping hand.

I magnified
what I *didn't* have,
believing it was more important
than what I *did* have.

I was at times hardhearted,
inflexible and uncaring
when disagreements arose.

I undermined
her feeling of security
by threatening to leave her.

I was trapped in the illusion
that patience,
surrender and generosity
were signs of weakness.

I failed to grasp
that almost all relationships
can be made to work,
through understanding
and a deep commitment
and unconditional love
for the other person.

After years of disappointment
and suffering,
I finally decided that
the indirect route
was not leading me
to the love and oneness
I longed for.

Demanding less

I finally saw the illusion
of having my happiness
depend on controlling
my partner's behavior.

I had to admit
that the most direct route
to my happiness
was, in fact, basic:

I create love in my heart
by what I tell myself—
by what I reject or accept.

My love comes from me!

And then I understood
how my use of power
eroded the love
in my own heart—
as well as
in my partner's heart.

I needed to learn
how to be more flexible
even when I think I'm right!

I started this process
back to love and unity
by becoming aware of the ways
in which I had
prevented myself from loving.

I learned
how my mind worked
and then devoted myself
to changing the mental habits
that had led to my separateness.

This meant initiating
and maintaining
new ways of thinking and reacting
which could create an experience
nearer to my heart's desire.

$\mathcal{I}$ found ways
of loving more and demanding less
that help a relationship work.

These were things
that I could do
and that did not require
my partner to work on herself.

I stopped worrying about 50-50:
"I'll do it if you do it."
"You had your way last time—
now it's my turn!"

I quit depending on my partner
to change
so I could enjoy
a loving relationship.

I want to share with you
how I learned
to break through
the mental habits
that made me feel irritation,
frustration and anger,
that destroyed the love,
appreciation and oneness
that I now know
can be created and sustained
in a relationship.

3

The Trap
of the Mind

Your world
is what your mind
is programmed to notice
and remember.

31

At any moment
you observe only
a fraction
of what's observable.

At any moment
you remember
only a fragment
of what there is to remember.

Using your special set of rules,
your mind automatically selects
what is acceptable or desirable
from the mass of data
reaching your senses.

Thus, your mind
creates an experience
that is projected
on the here and now.

You then identify
this highly abstracted,
incomplete experience
as "what is."

You lean
on this creation
of your mind
as a reliable guide
to what is real.

And this is how
you constantly live—
in a world
of self-created illusion.

This is a basic point
in the science of perception.

33

There may be a world of difference
in how you and your partner
interpret each event.

It will depend on which set
of emotional demands
and expectations
each of you
brings into focus
in every moment.

When there is conflict
and tension between you,
observe in each instance
what it is
you are demanding.

Formulate specifically
what you tell yourself
you will not accept.

Pay attention
to what seems to trigger
your displeasure.

Is it the timing?

Do you expect your beloved
to be amorous and romantic
when you first wake up
in the morning?

Or are you a late-nighter
who feels unloved and undesirable
because your partner falls asleep
without making love?

Is it a difference in habits?

You may insist that
your comfort depends
on your home being well organized,
while your partner spreads clothes
and papers around the house
with a nonchalant disregard
for your ideals of neatness.

Do you feel hurt
when your partner
is critical or discourteous
toward your friends?

Have you discovered
"insurmountable" differences
that you never
would have expected
in *your* beloved?

Have you created a battleground
around your individual tastes—
in clothes, foods, room temperature,
activities and interior decorating?

Do you feel
it means something about *you*
when your partner
wears sloppy clothes
or hangs a cheap print
next to your Picasso etching?

Does it mean
that s/he is unloving
when s/he insists
on seeing a different movie
from the one you had hoped
to see that evening?

In each of these cases
it is *your* demand or expectation
that is causing *your* feelings
of disappointment,
irritation and annoyance—
not what is actually happening.

If you did not *demand*
sex at a certain time,
or *your* choice of movie,
or *your* standard of orderliness,
you would understand
that the differences
between your values and timing
say nothing about you as a person—
they mean nothing
about either of you.

Instead of interpreting
the differences
as monumental obstacles,
as a lack of love
and understanding,
as intentional insults,
or as proof of incompatibility,
you can experience those differences
as caused only by models
you hold onto
in your mind.

Thus, it becomes easier
to understand at a deep level
that life situations
in themselves
do not make you
experience unhappiness
unless you resist them
and insist
that they be different.

41

You don't have to blame
your partner or yourself.

You are both innocent.

It is the rigid models
in your mind
that ultimately create
your experience of unhappiness!!!

It is in your power
to create happiness
by relaxing your models,
by learning to be flexible
and emotionally accepting for now
what life may be offering you.

You have the ability
to consciously survey
each here-and-now situation
in your life.

As you uplevel your demands
into preferences
by retraining your mental habits,
you stop being a robot.

You no longer automatically react
to life situations
by making yourself miserable
when your wishes
are not met.

What a miracle!

You can create a new experience
of your relationship.

You can escape
the traps of the mind
by transforming
your mental habits.

Now let's meet
the main players
within yourself
and learn to watch
the roles they have adopted.

44

4

The Separate-self

The Separate-self sees your life
as a struggle of "me vs. you."

With its excuses and defenses,
it keeps you self-centered
and self-conscious,
creating loneliness,
alienation, division
and the experience of "not enough."

It is that part of you
which deems itself
more important
than your openhearted part,
which wants to love
and understand your partner.

It's your Separate-self
that makes it more important
to feed your ego and show off
than to take time
to listen and be patient
with your partner.

Your mind is quite clever
at turning Separate-self desires
into "needs."

It sees the whole construction
of demands, expectations and "needs"
as normal and necessary,
not realizing that unhappiness
becomes the bitter fruit
of its inflexibility
and nonnegotiable requirements.

47

When your Separate-self takes over,
your partner's
constructive suggestions,
good intentions,
caring actions
and desire to love you
are hidden from
your awareness.

The Separate-self lets a veil
of fear, distrust and disappointment
harden to impenetrable walls
between you and your partner.

These walls are
the real obstacles
to creating a fulfilling
and enjoyable relationship.

49

As you start tearing down
the boundaries of your Separate-self
you will realize
that you and your partner
are lovable
just the way you are.

You will come in contact
with your love and appreciation
for yourself and your beloved
which has always existed
behind those walls.

You do not need the façade
your Separate-self
has tried to build up
to "protect" you.

The secret of
creating love in your life
is to know
that the Separate-self
is not your *true* self.

Begin to notice
the thoughts and actions
created by
your Separate-self.

You already have the means
to diminish
its harmful influence
as you allow
your Unified-self
to awaken.

51

5

The Unified-self

The Unified-self
is the golden core within you
that is generous, patient
and tunes-in to the oneness
between you and your partner.

52

It always knows
that, in your essence,
you are beautiful,
capable and lovable—
no matter how unskillfully
you may think or act
in any given scenario of life.

It is the part that can quiet
your racing mind
and take time to listen.

It is willing to be nonreactive
to any of your lover's
Separate-self words and actions
and to quietly find
the unity between you.

Your Unified-self within you
knows that it is
in giving
that you receive.

It knows that love
is more important
than any of your differences—
no matter how great
the Separate-self
perceives them to be.

The Unified-self
opens you to sharing
rather than hoarding.

It allows you
to integrate and harmonize with
the wishes of your partner
rather than oppose them
in a self-defensive way.

It approaches situations
in a wholistic manner—
and does not perceive the world
in terms of opposing interests.

A sage was asked,
"What is the beginning
of understanding?"

"To separate
one thing from another,"
he replied.

"And, what
is the beginning
of wisdom?"

"To see a unity
in everything."

Now, let's suppose
that you want to spend more time
with your lover
than s/he wants
to share with you.

Can you see beyond the duality?

There's you,
who wants to get closer,
and the "other"
who backs away from involvement,
who is not ready
for that much closeness.

Do you feel separate
and focus on blaming your beloved
for his/her feelings,
for not giving you
what you want
in the relationship?

The highest wisdom
sees everything
as a passing phase
in our journey of awakening
as we progress
from creating the Separate-self
to the more continuous joy
of the Unified-self.

Demanding less

6

Creating Oneness

Your mind can use
some assistance
in finding the way
back to the Unified-self
and the oneness
in your union.

When your Separate-self
creates the perception
of "me-vs.-you,"
quietly tell your mind
"not two."

Your partner wastes money—
tell yourself,
"not two."

Your partner
is overly friendly to someone els
say silently inside,
"not two."

Your partner
doesn't want sex tonight
when you want it—
"not two."

Your partner
wants sex tonight
and you don't—
"not two."

The highest wisdom
sees everything
as a passing phase
in our journey of awakening
as we progress
from creating the Separate-self
to the more continuous joy
of the Unified-self.

57

6

Creating Oneness

Your mind can use
some assistance
in finding the way
back to the Unified-self
and the oneness
in your union.

When your Separate-self
creates the perception
of "me-vs.-you,"
quietly tell your mind
"not two."

Your partner wastes money—
tell yourself,
"not two."

Your partner
is overly friendly to someone else,
say silently inside,
"not two."

Your partner
doesn't want sex tonight
when you want it—
"not two."

Your partner
wants sex tonight
and you don't—
"not two."

ow, let's suppose
that you want to spend more time
with your lover
than s/he wants
to share with you.

Can you see beyond the duality?

There's you,
who wants to get closer,
and the "other"
who backs away from involvement,
who is not ready
for that much closeness.

Do you feel separate
and focus on blaming your beloved
for his/her feelings,
for not giving you
what you want
in the relationship?

What would it feel like
to create the experience
of oneness
in this situation?

First, mentally draw
one large circle
and place both you
and your partner
inside this circle.

This is the "us" circle.

61

Now re-experience the scene:
one of US wants more involvement,
another of US
wants more space.

From a mountaintop perspective
can you sense that
in the essence of oneness
it doesn't matter emotionally
who is playing which role?

By drawing a mental circle
around both of you,
you create a feeling
that both of you
are in this game together.

It is not a matter
of winning or losing.

It's "you *and* me,"
not "you *vs.* me."

No blaming yourself
or your partner.

No separateness.

No judgmentalness.

No criticism.

Just accepting what's now
and doing whatever is needed
to live out
the next act
in the drama of your life.

At times you have created
the experience of oneness
with your beloved.

You can reclaim
and keep that feeling
of togetherness and love.

There is no need
to throw your partner
out of your heart—
even temporarily!

Whenever your partner
does or says
anything you don't like,
your life is giving you
an opportunity
to get some practice
in developing your skill
to love unconditionally—
to create the oneness—
and let go of the two-ness.

65

Can you understand and accept
if your partner
spends time
with someone else?

Can your love
stretch so wide
that it encircles
all three of you?

When you back off
and give space to your beloved,
s/he may surprise you
by becoming more affectionate
and attentive to you.

The power and antagonism of
"you AGAINST me"
destroys love.

The understanding,
compassion and cooperativeness
of "you AND me"
opens the heart
to loving.

You create a mutual reality
that becomes deeper and deeper
and strengthens your experience
as a couple.

Demanding less

Be patient with yourself.

You have a lifetime
of mental habits
that often distort
the way you perceive
what's around you.

Your ego and your mind
have been trapped in boxes
that make you perceive
the "two-ness"
in many life situations.

These insidious separating habits
often keep you
from getting in touch
with your Unified-self—
even when you deeply want to.

Always remember—
you are retraining
your mind and heart
to perceive
the oneness in situations
FOR YOUR OWN BENEFIT.

Don't wait to make a deal:
"I'll create the oneness
if you do, too."

Your partner may remain stuck
in separateness and alienation—
at least for now.

Work only on
your own Separate-self.

Your partner will sense
your loving space
when you uplevel into preferences
the demands that trigger
anger and resentment in you.

As you do your inner work,
you will be less likely
to activate in your partner
his or her demands
that result in
feelings of fear,
frustration and anger.

hus,
by working only
on your own Separate-self,
you can assist your partner
in touching his/her own
self-acceptance and love—
and this love
will then be projected back
to you!

This is one of the secrets
for creating
a wonderful relationship.

Demanding less

Your relationship is your mirror.

IT	IT
REFLECTS	REFLECTS
YOU	YOU
BACK	BACK
TO	TO
YOU!	YOU!

f your Separate-self
has been in the habit
of resenting your partner,
are you surprised
when you are resented
in return?

Or, to put it another way—
if you plant cactus,
you get cactus.

If you plant zinnias,
you get zinnias.

If you plant love,
you get love.

You have always known
that it works this way—
and still you keep on forgetting.

Demanding less

Have patience . . .
Many of your heart's desires
will be realized,
as you increasingly
open yourself
to the unfolding
of your Unified-self.

A flower opens into full bloom
when it is ready.

So will your love blossom . . . .

Be gentle with yourself—
and your beloved.

75

Love
Without Strings

LOVE
IS THE MOST
POWERFUL BOND
THAT EXISTS
BETWEEN PEOPLE!

Nothing else
is capable of integrating
and harmonizing
your complex energies
and desires
that otherwise
may keep you trapped
in separateness and alienation—
forever in conflict.

 **"REAL"
LOVE
IS
UNCONDITIONAL
LOVE.**

**"No matter what
you say or do—
I just go on
loving you."**

Unconditional love
doesn't mean
you have to like everything
your partner says or does.

Your partner is not
his or her actions—
any more than you are
what you say or do.

You can allow yourself
to appreciate the actor or actress
even if you don't like
the role
s/he is playing
in this movie.

Demanding less

Both you and your partner
are always lovable
even when you act
unkindly or unwisely—
just as a child
is lovable
even when
s/he is noisy
or mischievous.

re you
giving your relationship
the benefit of
the incredibly powerful energy
of UNCONDITIONAL LOVE?

Or are you crippling
your relationship
with a diluted form
of love?

"I'll love you if—"
is love with a hook.

Demanding less

If you feel love
for your partner
only when s/he is meeting
your models, desires
and expectations,
it will become obvious
that your love is conditional
and undependable.

That's not pure love—
it's a barter, an exchange:
"I'll act nice
and love you,
if you behave
as I want you to,
but watch out—
if you don't do what I want
I may take my love away."

Conditional love
perpetuates the consciousness
of the Separate-self—
when your heart
is only intermittently
and incompletely
loving your partner.

Your conditional love
will most likely
be mirrored back to you
by your partner.

Conditional love limits.

**It limits your insight,
your energy,
your happiness,
your joy,
and your feeling of purpose
and oneness
in the relationship.**

Your unconditional love will grow
as you become more sensitive
and skillful in understanding
the messages you and your partner
send to each other.

You can learn to sift out
the separating defensive games
and tune-in to the same yearning
for love and acceptance
within both of you.

ONLY YOUR OWN
UNCONDITIONAL LOVE
CAN LEAD YOU
TO YOUR HEART'S DESIRE.

8

The Hidden
Yearning

You will find new insights
with which to nurture
a growth and expansion
in yourself and your beloved,
when you look for
the positive intentions
on the part
of both of you.

87

For both of you,
your deep desire
for love and acceptance
is all too often disguised.

Now become a miner
for the nuggets of love
that lie buried under layers
of diversionary activities.

Suppose you make yourself
feel disappointed, irritated
and frustrated
and lash out in angry words
and actions
when your partner spends time
on hobbies that you don't share.

You need not assume
that your partner is escaping
from your relationship
or is purposely ignoring
your desires
for your life together.

You could look
at the situation
in a new
and more creative way.

You could have the insight
that your partner's activities
do not by themselves
create your irritation.

Your irritation is caused
solely by your patterns of mind,
by your own expectations
which find your partner's behavior
unacceptable.

What might be
your underlying
positive intentions
for lashing out
at your partner?

Perhaps you lash out
in the hope that your partner
will change his/her habits,
realizing how they upset you.

Of course you have
little or no control
over how your partner
will react.

And you already know
that your partner's behavior
does not necessarily make you happy
or unhappy—
your expectations
play a determining part
in creating *your* experience.

The intentions you are looking for
can best be found
by asking yourself
how you would feel
if your partner
changed his/her behavior,
if s/he were, for example,
devoting more attention to you.

91

ou might feel relaxed.
You might feel more supported.
You might feel more loved
and more loving.

Let's say that
your desire to feel loved
is your positive intention—
or ultimate goal.

Your lashing out at your partner
is an *unskillful* attempt
to feel loved.

Will it bring you the love
that is your positive intention
in this case?

Have you ever been able
to get your partner
to feel closer to you
when your Separate-self
angrily and bitingly criticizes?

Have you found
acting out "me vs. you"
to be a productive way
to get your partner to change?

It may sometimes seem to work,
but at the price of separation
and resentment.

If you look carefully
you can find more effective ways
to enable yourself
to feel loved.

You can find
creative options and alternatives
instead of pounding away
with what doesn't work.

Tune-in to your own inner wisdom.

The creative and loving parts
of your Unified-self
can inspire alternate methods.

You may choose
to remind yourself quietly
over and over again:
"I am enough."
"I am lovable."
"It means nothing about me."
"I can accept . . .
(whatever you are objecting to)."

This practice
may in time
alter your belief systems.

ou also always have the choice
of finding your own interests
and goals
that could help you feel
loved and fulfilled.

Observe
that it is your own
positive intentions
we are talking about,
your own feelings,
the internal experience
that you can initiate and maintain
independent of the outside world.

You can also practice
looking for
the positive intentions
motivating your partner's behavior.

If your partner
devotes more time to hobbies
than you'd like,
what might be
his/her positive intentions?

Perhaps s/he feels
stifled on the job
and seeks to be envigorated
by jogging or fishing.

Maybe s/he wants to maintain
the strong bonds of old friendships
by playing golf or tennis.

A creative hobby
may fill a desire
for expression
of his/her inner being.

It can be a wish for solitude
and contemplation
in a world
of noise and pressure.

Behind all these
positive intentions
there may be another
even more basic
positive intention or goal—
his/her yearning
for love and appreciation.

Now you could find
creative new ways
to help in the achievement
of these intentions
of your partner.

You could contribute love
and energy
to the positive intentions,
rather than adding
barbed remarks and resentment!

In each moment
you can give your partner
the same compassion and insight
that you seek for yourself.

Ask yourself,
"What feelings
am I really longing for?"

Know that both you
and your partner
share the same
dream of love.

**IF YOU LOOK FAR ENOUGH
YOU'LL ALWAYS FIND
A POSITIVE, BENEFICIAL INTENTION
BEHIND *ALL* HUMAN BEHAVIOR.**

Don't keep pounding away
with demands
that create separateness.

Leap over the "impossible issues"
and tune-in to
the underlying positive intentions
of both you and your partner.

This opens you
to find new ways
to make life work together.

There is a *basic goodness*
within each person.

There is a *basic goodness*
that may be implemented
by unskillful ways.

Behind all separating acts
there are always
positive, worthwhile intentions.

Even when people
do horrendous things
they are just trying
in unskillful ways
to make their lives work.

The problem is not
that they are bad or evil—
they just need new ways.

They need the insights
of creative new options
to realize their positive intentions
to feel good, lovable and loved,
to get on with their lives.

Demanding less

9

Letting Go

Your life works better
when you realize
that your happiness
does not have to depend
on changing your partner.

You always have the choice
to try to influence
what your partner says or does.

But another option is available
and within your immediate ability—
letting go of your demands.

That involves the insight
that most of the things you demand
are just not worth the penalties
in alienation
and lost love
that you are creating.

Letting go
involves an internal shift
in your emotions.

It is the difference
between *demanding*
that something be different
and *preferring*
that it be different.

It is being willing
to *emotionally* accept
the here-and-now
life situation.

You can create this shift
by listening attentively,
and by changing
your internal dialogue
and mental habits.

This is like giving
your hot nagging mind
a cool bath.

Demanding less

It takes mental strength,
patience,
courage and determination
to emotionally let go.

It often means forgiving
and forgetting
things your partner
has done or said.

By giving up
your mental expectations
that things always be
exactly the way you want,
you can begin to enjoy life
the way it is.

Letting go can be much easier
and more effective
than continuously
fighting and resisting
"what is."

Demanding less

The desire to be right—
to judge what is "good" or "bad"
are traps of the Separate-self.

Your mind can almost always
find reasons why
what you want
is right or fair.

And you are
not alone—
your partner
is bound
to do the same.

Even if you *are right*
and you *are sure*
that fairness
is all on your side,
be willing to do
the inner work necessary.

In each situation ask yourself:
"What do I think I get
by hanging on?
What am I avoiding?
What is the danger of letting go?
What would it take
for me to let go?"

When you can understand
the price you pay in lost love,
you can more easily let go
of the emotional upset,
of your unrealized desires,
expectations and demands!

Demanding less

Look back on your relationships.

Can you see how you both
could have won
if you would have
just let go?

Could you have stopped
pushing your partner into dieting
to meet your models
of body shape or health?

How would it have felt
if you had refrained from sarcasm
when s/he reached
for the third drink
or the second cream puff?

How would you have both felt,
if you had just
let each other be what you were,
accepting each other
as individual human beings
without resisting and clinging
to your models of
how it ought to be?

Can you understand
that it was only
your models and desires
that stood between you
and your happiness?

Sometimes your ego-mind
prevents you from understanding
what is involved
in letting go
of a demand.

Letting go
does not necessarily mean
that you have to decide
that you are "wrong"
about your point of view.

When you go from
demanding to preferring,
you can still
believe you're right.

It just means that you stop
making yourself feel
emotionally separate
when you don't get
what you want.

It means growing
in the realization
of what truly counts
in the relationship—
love, cooperation
and the many benefits
of creating together
the great adventure
of life!

115

ou can still put energy
into changing
what is changeable,
but you do not lose
your health
and enjoyment of life
by making yourself upset
in the meantime.

By letting go
you no longer
disturb your serenity
when the world
does not meet
the insistent models
in your head.

By letting go
you stop pushing
your emotional buttons
of fear, frustration and anger.

Life will never
meet all your models,
expectations and desires.

It never has!

It never will!

117

Don't play martyr:
"I'm right—you're wrong,
but I'll give in to show you
how fair I am."

You may successfully
manipulate your partner.

You may convince him/her
of your virtue and "sacrifice"
in the relationship,
but it's doubtful
that you will receive
what you most want—
a feeling of love.

Keeping score
in your mind
so that your partner
feels s/he
"owes you one"
can be another
self-defeating practice.

Demanding less

Don't let your rational mind
try to tell you
that you are being weak
and submissive
or losing your identity,
if you just let go
of your demands and desires.

"Never give in."
"Go down fighting."
"Don't be a coward."
"You're right. Tell her off."
"Teach him a lesson."

They are only unskillful
power points of view
inherited from
our jungle past.

Consider before letting go,
"Is this something
that is essential
or is it a demand
that I can truly afford
to let go?"

Give only
what you can afford
to give.

What if your partner
were to play music
at top volume
for hours at a time?

Would you be able to let go
of your demand
for more quiet?

Let's say
you just can't stand
the music.

If you didn't protest,
your resentment might build
tension and separation,
so you may choose
to take a stand.

When you are aware
of the happiness you may gain,
you may be amazed
at how often you *can* let go
of something seemingly important.

Letting go can offer
an instant return
of love and unity
in your heart
anytime you do it!

Isn't that preferable
to staying locked
in the "me-vs.-you" conflict
of your desire systems?

Demanding less

Now is the time
to open your heart
and love more
than ever before!

Try doing
what you want
your partner to do.

If you want your partner
to be more patient,
then *you* be more patient.

Don't wait for
your partner
to do it first—
you could have
a long wait!

But it will not work
if you let your ego
just pretend
to give up
the separating demands.

The power of love
will work for you only
when you can truly let go.

By channeling your energy
from your Separate-self
to your Unified-self,
your life will work better.

It will increase
your emotional flexibility.

You can simultaneously
be a participant
and an observer
in the game of life.

You will integrate
your head
and your heart.

Doing so
can cause
a glorious transformation
of your life!

10

Love in Action

LOVE HAS THE POWER
TO MAKE UNIMPORTANT
ALL THE DIFFERENCES
BETWEEN YOU!!!

Demanding less

LOVE LETS YOU CREATE
A HAPPY EXPERIENCE OF LIFE,
EVEN WHEN YOU DISAGREE.

LOVE ALLOWS YOU TO DISAGREE
IN AN AGREEABLE MANNER!

LOVE HELPS YOU GO BEYOND
THE PRISON OF YOUR SEPARATE-SELF
INTO CREATING THE HAPPINESS
OF YOUR UNIFIED-SELF!

Real love
involves tearing down
the many barriers
that keep you
feeling separate
from your beloved.

As your Unified-self
deepens your love,
you begin to care more.

You want your partner's life
to work well for him or her.

You increasingly become committed
both to your relationship
and to loving and serving
your partner.

Be kind to yourself.

When your old nagging habits
start emerging,
fill your mind with
compassion, harmony and delight.

Have compassion for yourself
and your partner.

The suffering
in your hearts
often feels caused by reality,
but it is based
on illusions.

Be determined to reprogram your mind
so that you no longer
will have to put up
with its insatiable tendencies—
its constant demands for more . . . .

Tell your mind to be happy
with "enough"!

No one *ever*
gets it all!

131

Your Unified-self
can develop a strength
which no insistent demand
can ever overwhelm
or conquer.

Use this strength
to protect and nurture
your vision of harmony.

Look with delight
at what *is*
in your relationship.

Instead of feeling deprived
of what you don't have,
ask yourself,
"Do I have enough to be happy?"

Your insights may pierce
the veil of illusion
and expose the abundance
that you *do* have
here and now.

Bring oneness
to your union
by making gentle suggestions,
with loving undertones.

Treasure those qualities
that exhibit the best
in your partner.

Among these are the values
that originally
brought you together.

Blaming can only separate.
The result is far too costly.

Let your Separate-self cool off
so you can hear the messages
from your Unified-self
that will give you new insights
into your recent argument.

Tune-in to the positive intentions
of yourself and your partner
to fulfill your yearning
for cooperation and love
within your relationship.

Work on yourself quietly,
without trying to manipulate,
and without expectations.

Find the areas
where you need to let go.
Enter ever-deeper levels
of commitment
to let go of your demands
which keep you stuck in pride,
insecurity and resentment.

Can you find ways
to let yourself feel good
without changing
anything outside of you?

Demanding less

Recommit yourself
to your relationship
every day anew.

Risk being vulnerable.

Share your deepest thoughts
without laying blame.

"I know it is my programming,
but I feel humiliated
when you tell those old jokes
to our new friends."

"I don't want you to know
that I am always so willing to help
because it feeds my desire
to be needed—
to be praised."

"Yes, I need praise.
I would like you to thank me
when I do something special for you,
yet I feel ashamed
to feel that needy."

"I don't dare let you know
how dependent on you I feel—
how much you mean to me,
because I'm afraid
that will give you
too much power over me."

"I am afraid to tell you
that I feel attracted to Bill
but I don't want to hide from you."

Demanding less

All the while
be aware of why you are sharing.
If it is to make yourself
feel superior,
for daring to be braver
than your partner,
it is not likely
to give you the results
you long for.

You're sharing to increase
the cooperation and love
between you and your partner.

Sharing from a right/wrong,
"me-vs.-you" space
may or may not give you
the results you long for.

But when you share
with love in your heart
your sharing
will help you feel closer
to your loved one.

Even when your intention
is to shatter the illusion
of separateness
and bring closeness,
it may take many attempts
and a lot of patience
as you open your heart
day by day.

Demanding less

The road to happiness
involves deep honesty
with yourself
and a willingness to share
your goals and outlook
with your lover.

The more you know who you are
and where you want to go,
the more solid
is your love for yourself,
and your ability to survive
the differences and tensions
in your relationship.

$\mathcal{O}$pen yourself honestly:
"This is how I feel.
This is what I like."

Risk expressing your caring
in actions and in words,
even if you do not think
your partner will respond
in like manner.

Be the first one to say:
"I love you,"—
and keep on saying it . . . .

Reaching out with love
and touching and hugging
will enrich and strengthen
your own being.

141

Find the rhythms
and rituals
that will enrich
your union.

As you open yourself to abundance,
you can begin to see your life
from a broader perspective,
and see the humor
in your own personal drama.

11

Remembering the Choice

Each moment
you have a choice:
be happy or suffer.

It is up to you!

Your partner, and the world,
may continue to be as they are
but you can choose
to liberate yourself
from judgmental thoughts,
from fear
and from impatience.

Letting go
is a gift to yourself
of more energy,
insight, love
and peace of mind,
and less strain and stress
on your body.

When you start
feeling upset,
remind yourself of your choice—
"I find it more fulfilling
to be loving
than to insist
on being right."

Use phrases
that will guide your mind:

"I can accept
that Annie forgot our anniversary."

"I can love myself
when John wants to spend
time alone with his children."

"It doesn't mean
anything about me
when Eric has standards
that I don't meet."

Demanding less

No more helplessly hoping
that the situation automatically
will right itself.

You are the artist who,
moment by moment,
is creating
your internal emotional experience
of your relationship.

Use your rich inner resources—
go back in time and relive
some treasured moments
when life was wonderful:
see the scene,
hear the voices and sounds,
remember textures and touch,
feel the warm glow within.

That is just as real
as the misery
you often let yourself feel.

You have a deep well
of joy within.

Drink from it
and be healed.

Demanding less

Once you taste success,
your skill will grow
in consciously de-escalating
your desire systems.

As you accept
the previously "unacceptable,"
your love will deepen.

As your love deepens
you will more easily
let go of more demands—
and thus increase
your unconditional love.

This transformation
can heal you
and our strife-torn world.

We each have the potential
to create our experience—
of ourselves,
of our partners,
of other people
and of the world around us
through filters of love.

We can deepen
our compassion
for the dilemma
and collective suffering
of this beloved earth
and the roles
we all play.

We have the power to transcend
our Separate-selves.

We are all human beings
with similar hopes and needs.
We are meant
to enjoy the beauty
of our Unified-selves.

149

When we achieve the insight
that there is no one to blame,
we are in a position of openness—
prepared for the miracle of rebirth,
ready for maturity
and oneness.

Humanity has reached
the point of choice:

Do we let our differences
and disagreements
destroy our relationships?

Or will we learn
how to deepen our insights
to harmonize,
to cooperate,
to quietly grow in love,
to tune-in
to the gift of life
and the cosmic humor
and adventure of it all?

Demanding less

Is there any higher priority
for any of us—
and for all of humanity?

Let's spread the good news:

We can work together.

We can open our hearts together.

We will win the game of life—
together.

Demanding less

TOGETHER
WE CAN CREATE
OUR LIVES
NEARER TO
OUR HEART'S DESIRE!

Appendix 1

THE KEN KEYES CENTER

The Ken Keyes Center, in Coos Bay, Oregon, is the headquarters for three activities offering loving service to you:

CLEARMIND TRAININGS: These trainings are designed for people who want practical help in increasing the love and happiness in their lives. Offered at nonprofit prices, they enable you to benefit from our experience in teaching the Science of Happiness. The trainings include weekend, week-long, two-week and month-long programs. They are available at Coos Bay and from time to time in various cities throughout the United States. A free catalog may be obtained from ClearMind Trainings, 790 Commercial Avenue, Coos Bay, OR 97420, phone (503) 267-6412.

VISION CENTERS: These are local centers that meet on the first and third Tuesday evening of each month in many of the larger cities. They operate on a community basis and provide ongoing support in deepening your understanding of the skills discussed in this book. These meetings give you the opportunity to meet others who wish to grow in creativity, love, happiness and the feeling of purpose in their lives. One of the highlights of each meeting is a new videotape of Ken or one of the ClearMind trainers. You are invited to be a free guest for your first meeting. For information on the location of the Vision Center nearest you, write or phone Vision Centers, 790 Commercial Avenue, Coos Bay, OR 97420, phone (503) 267-4415.

LIVING LOVE PUBLICATIONS: This is the central publishing and distribution office for all of the books by Ken Keyes. In addition, cassettes are produced from workshops and interviews, as well as music tapes of the songs used in the trainings.

All of Ken's books are priced so you can afford to give them to your friends. The next section describes his books that are now available.

Appendix 2

OTHER BOOKS BY KEN KEYES, JR.

Handbook to Higher Consciousness, $3.95
This is the basic text in the Living Love Way for getting the most out of your life. It is literally a handbook that gives you directions for creating a happy, loving life. It explains six methods you can choose from to help you increase your enjoyment. Countless people have experienced dramatic change from the time they began to use these practical methods.

A Conscious Person's Guide to Relationships, $3.95
Here, finally, is love without tears! A must for people who want love in their lives. This breakthrough book has a unique approach with helpful guidelines for entering into a relationship, for being in one, or for decreasing the involvement without bitterness and recriminations. It is enjoyable to read, realistic in its approach and immensely helpful if you have a relationship or wish to find one. It will show you how to gradually create the high level of love and enjoyment you've wanted to share with the person you live with.

How to Enjoy Your Life in Spite of It All, $4.95
Each of the Twelve Pathways is thoroughly explained in this book. Ken (who formulated the Twelve Pathways) offers you his detailed insights into these guidelines for creating a more enjoyable life. Step by step, he shows you how to take the Pathways from the printed page and make them dynamic tools for bringing increased energy, perceptiveness, love and inner peace into your day-to-day living.

Prescriptions for Happiness, $2.95
Treat yourself to more happiness by having these prescriptions handy! This book can help you tune-in to effective techniques to create an enriched life. A perfect gift to yourself or anyone else you treasure.

Taming Your Mind, $7.95
This enjoyable book (which has been in print for 30 years) shows you how to use your mind more effectively. It contains about 80 full-page drawings by the famous illustrator Ted Key. It is written in a deeply effective but entertaining style. It was previously published under the title *How to Develop Your Thinking Ability*. It was adopted by two book clubs and has sold over 100,000 copies.

How to Make Your Life Work or Why Aren't You Happy? by Ken Keyes, Jr. and Bruce Burkan, $2.95
This book is fun to read! Every other page is a delightful, to-the-point cartoon that adds meaning to the timely message. You may find that this simple, enjoyable book offers you what you've been missing to enable your life to be really great!

The Hundredth Monkey, $2.00
There is no cure for nuclear war—ONLY PREVENTION! This book points out the unacceptability of nuclear weapons for human health. It challenges you to take a new look at your priorities. With the intriguing new concept about the power of our combined efforts, it shows how you can dispel old myths and create a new vision to save humanity.

Available through bookstores or from Living Love Publications, 790 Commercial Ave., Coos Bay, OR 97420, (503) 267-4112. Please enclose $1.25 for each $10 worth of books for postage and packaging.